"With aplomb and arresting originality of language, Joanne
Nelson bears witness to the complex relationship between trou-
bled family legacies and self-determination. *My Neglected Gods* is a
record of the compassion for self—and ultimately for family—that
comes with clear seeing."

JOANNA PENN COOPER, AUTHOR OF
THE ITINERANT GIRL'S GUIDE TO SELF-HYPNOSIS

"Ancestors and heirs, neighbors and siblings—they punctuate
Joanne Nelson's moving collection of essays, *My Neglected Gods*.
I remember the characters in this book because each one is
revealed through precise heart-wrenching detail: the 'carefully
tucked paisley sheets' of a mother's bed, 'shadow selves' left in
the 'damp imprint' of towels, the neighbor who tells everyone
about the metal plate in his head, the other neighbor who leans
on Nelson's mailbox, catching his breath, not long before he
dies, a baby who points at bunnies and Goldfish crackers. There's
sadness here, and grief and regret. But there's also appreciation
and gratitude and attentiveness. More than anything, this collection of meditative essays is characterized by an assurance Nelson
experienced during a mystical connection with her deceased
grandmother: everything is going to be all right."

LYNN DOMINA, AUTHOR OF *FRAMED IN SILENCE*

"There is so much life in the pages of *My Neglected Gods* the book
feels like one of those magic capsules that expands into a dinosaur
when you drop them in a glass of water. The vignettes may be
miniature in scale, and composed with elegant precision, but they
contain entire worlds. Joanne Nelson is a writer of real heart and
exquisite control."

BENJAMIN ANASTAS, AUTHOR OF *TOO GOOD TO BE TRUE*

About the Author

Joanne Nelson is the author of the memoir, *This Is How We Leave*. Her writing appears in numerous journals and anthologies. She won the Hal Prize in nonfiction, as well as other literary awards, and has contributed to Lake Effect on Milwaukee's NPR station. Nelson lives in Hartland, Wisconsin, where she teaches at the university level and leads community programs. She gives presentations on mindfulness and writing, creativity, and the second half of life. Nelson holds an MFA from the Bennington Writing Seminars, an MSSW from the University of Wisconsin-Madison, and is a certified meditation instructor.

More information is available at
wakeupthewriterwithin.com

MY NEGLECTED GODS

JOANNE NELSON

www.vineleavespress.com

Print Edition
ISBN: 978-3-98832-016-2
Published by Vine Leaves Press 2023

Cover design by Jessica Bell
Interior design by Amie McCracken

For my family and friends.
You truly are the gods and goddesses in my life.

Contents

Author's Note

Many of the names in *My Neglected Gods* have been
changed to afford privacy to those involved. Other than
that, this memoir is as true as the vagaries of memory,
time, and experience allow. Any mistakes are my own.

Legacy

Leftovers

Mayonnaise,
      cream cheese,
            sun-dried tomatoes,
                  Thai peanut sauce. My visiting,
hungry daughter checks expiration dates and exhales
patience. One hand holds the refrigerator door open
and she bends at the waist to reach for each jar, long
hair falling over her shoulder. From my seat at the
kitchen counter, I analyze each item ahead of her hand,
calculating length of time since purchase.

This is how it begins. Soon the phrase, "You should
see what I found in her refrigerator ..." will pepper her
conversation with friends.

My mother's refrigerator, at the end of her indepen-
dence, contained, amongst other things: a saucepan
of chicken noodle soup—small moons of chicken fat
floating in the thin broth; plastic containers of gray-
brown fuzziness; and several half-cans of Pabst Blue
Ribbon beer. I tossed and tossed into white Hefty bags,
which I stacked next to the over-full garbage bin at the
end of her driveway.

No one witnessed the hunched muscles of my shoulders or the building tension in my face as I worked. But if my mother could escape her nursing home, could escape her failing self, I think she'd recognize this look—even be able to imitate it. I wore it so often in her presence.

The handle of my grandmother's Philco refrigerator demanded a hard pull before the loud, sticky door seal released to reveal half-eaten apple pie, gravy-soaked roast beef on a chipped flower-rimmed plate, and drying, unwrapped cheese on yet another chipped plate.

Every Sunday, her home filled with luscious smells and flavors, savory pies and meats. I ate and overate but avoided any leftovers if I visited during the week. Perhaps I was too cautious though—Grandma cooked for herself well into her nineties. She lived until my daughter grew in me, until I could reach into the refrigerator of my own home and bring out apples extra flavorful for having been kept cold and unsliced.

I remember the comforting edge of those broken plates, can see the dividing line where the border of the aging yellow/orange cheese faded to softness—where a thin paring knife could cut away anything unpleasant and save the rest for another time. I hear her say whatever I do to my mother I'll get back threefold.

I hear her say it again as I watch my girl, now so grown, so beautiful, turn from the refrigerator, jar in hand, like a punctuation mark of continuance or ending.

Still Life

"Dale," the restaurant's hostess calls and because it's been five years I don't look up. My brother's that dead and no hostess will raise him or call him forth to claim one last omelet. I'd like to see him cross the foyer of rustling people-filled benches though, have him share in this Sunday morning buzzing energy. Hear him complain about the wait, feel his pockets for smokes, say "don't give me that look" before stepping outside. I want to call his name, say it out loud like the hostess says it: quick and easy. Dale. Hey Dale, what are you doing? Dale, want to come over? Dale, can I come over? Dale will you, can you?

A bleak, watery day the last time I drove north and then further north to his cabin in the woods, desperate to see the state of his life or non-life for myself. He didn't rise from the one comfortable chair when I walked in, didn't turn his head to offer welcome or hello. A still life: barefoot, shirt but no pants, beer bottles and cigarettes and ashtray within reach. Even the smells suspended, unwashed, motionless. Piled mail. The place hazy with cigarette smoke. I watched him light the wrong end of a cigarette and take a puff and another puff before turning it around. His tired, unkempt, also hazy-with-cigarette-smoke dog a shadow next to his chair.

Scrambled egg hunks amongst the unwashed plates in the sink, the grimy knives and forks. I boiled the flatware—it was that bad, scrubbed the rest so I could make him a meal: chicken and rice to make everything nice again. I picked through and tossed the gunk so the drain could run clear. He didn't remember making eggs, he told me. Thought he might have puked in the sink.

Dale Michael. Dale had a lopsided grin. Dale played catch with me. Dale grew up and married and worked and divorced and married and worked and divorced two more times, and just got tired of it all, I guess. Dale shot his dishwasher. Dale got pulled over. Dale this and Dale that. Dale said he wouldn't but did, and promised but didn't. Dale has a broken liver; Dale's kidneys don't work. Dale is almost sure who I am. Says, "sister." Pauses. "You're my sister."

He eats his napkin along with his pudding, he sees dancing girls in his room at night. He doesn't get better. Dale won't answer no matter how many times his name is called.

Covid Days

I forget sometimes. Just go about my business.
Writing, petting the dog, scooping ice cream.
Immersed.

Then the memory wave returns and I calculate
every step outside the door's possible cost.
Quick review of loved ones, of who's healing
and who isn't.

Self-assessment: Chills? Cough?

All day like this.

Here We Are
in the Photo Album

Picture my dead aunt Helen and me at a bar. She wants us to take a picture together, reaches for her cell phone and selfie stick but I say no, no thank you. Despite my refusal she's willing to clink our ice-cold mugs of beer together, then blow the heavy head of foam aside before sipping. "Ahh good," she says.

Oh to be with Helen! Such a smile she had! And always the popsicles in the freezer box. But there's not much chance for Helens anymore. I'll buy you a beer if you can bring me a breathing Helen; take her arm and help her out of some picture frame, have her offer me an orange popsicle. We'll find some sun-dusty tavern, plop ourselves down.

I'd like to see a few others pop out of the photo album and belly up to the bar. See that tall boy at my daughter's balloon-filled birthday party? His mom helping cut cake? Plane crash, both of them. Let's move on.

Look! There's my husband's father. On a red bike! We put his dog down last week. And as for him, well, the red bike hasn't been seen in a while. Maybe turn the page now. Grandmothers. Pages of grandmothers with pages of cakes. Here's my dad. Pabst in hand. Smiling. He fell while getting the yard ready for a party. Heart attack or fall on that sparkling autumn day—we'll never know which came first.

My dead mother makes regular appearances. She's in constant movement across the photo album, reaching for something, turning towards someone, leaning in, pouring this, slicing that. Laughing with Helen as she hands her an apple. There's me, pregnant with my second—no, no, that's my third—the second didn't live long enough to be born. And there's my godmother. She left us for the angels last year. My husband's mother, Barbara, still life with coffee at a long-ago kitchen table. Barbara. Another name for the dead. My daughter's godfather laughing at something off stage—we sure didn't see that coming. And my brother—well, we all saw that one coming.

Here's my newborn in the arms of her great-grandma. We were so lucky to get that photo! A few pages later the baby becomes a child goofing with her favorite cousin. She wears a pink dress. He wears a red bow tie. Both so bright-eyed. So young and sure. Holiday after holiday and page after page they stick their tongues out at the camera. No hint of tragedy shadows him across the crowded dining rooms and backyard patios of the photos.

Helen asks again about a photo together. But I see what happens; I shake my head no.

No thank you.

Rewriting the Mom Character

If I begin to embrace the way you brightened when I walked into a room, hear your voice call me lovely, or— without rolling my eyes—the way you boasted about me to the neighbors. There's the two of us at the library. The drawers of the card catalog you taught me to use, their quiet easy pulls, the musty smell of the stacks, low shh of librarians if we spoke a word, how each book tipped so easily into my hand. We'd nestle in the line-dried, carefully tucked paisley sheets of your bed, me with my *Little House* books, you with your magazines, background hum of the radio, bowl of potato chips between us, the dog hopeful at our feet.

If I remember the expensive electric typewriter—blue— with correctable ribbon cartridge you gave me when I left for college and then the raw silk, beautifully cut interview suit for graduation. Neither item handed down or on sale, both way beyond good enough. You defended me against bullies and brothers and the occasional nun, finished layer cakes with my favorite frosting, let me have the beaters, made extra to spread on graham crackers. All our meals were hot and the laundry done.

What if I unfold these images first, balance them equally with your faded robe and unbrushed hair as you lean over a drawer of pills, or with the beer bottles hidden under unused guest towels or even with the sound of your weeping?

Legacy

If I take a cup from the cupboard, perhaps
the blue-lipped one, mindful of the glued-on handle
—smoothed-over mistake—
does my cortex or whatever whisper directions?
Close your hand here, lift from the shelf now.
Does each action have a past?
What guides me through this yellow kitchen?
Am I my mother moving through hers,
only a color scheme apart?

My unwitting daughter believes the choices are still hers.

Wipe the counter clockwise, keep the towels hidden,
apples in a bowl, old coffee in a jar, napkins at the ready.
Coffee beans and a piece of chocolate in the freezer.
Your life is not your own. Just try cleaning
the counter this way instead of that.
Listen as the dishes crash.

Honeymoon

Puerto Vallarta's sticky heat spills from the photo along with the sounds of a mariachi band, of clinking glasses, of chairs scraping across the floor. There's a straw in one of the glasses, but the plates remain clean. Our gazes focus outward towards a house, kids, promotions. We'll finish our meal, I remember this, then walk back towards the hotel surrounded by voices we don't understand. The photo is in black and white as if we still wait for the colors to be turned on.

Preparation

In the basement my mother snaps towels into the air, brushes each one smooth against her body, folds and adds to the pile on the dryer humming with another load. She gives me hankies for practice. My hands too full of the season, I drop more than I fold before adding to my crooked hill.

"Don't get too excited," she warns, "you'll only be disappointed." I'm left with the enormity of this thing called *too*. The drone of the dryer sways everything ever so slightly. Christmas paper and tinsel scent the air. She straightens the folded towels, corrects my ragged edges before the hankies fall.

Too excited is a risk I'm willing to take.

Shadow Selves

Loud. Happy. Connie, Lisa, and I chased each other through backyard lawn sprinklers. Then, costumed in our mothers' oldest bath towels we headed for the sun-warmed front sidewalk. We rested. Cheeks on folded hands. Imprints of our hip bones, forearms, thighs visible each time we moved our towels to another, dryer spot.

We traveled down the block this way, stopping only at the corner. The curb the end of our freedom. Too soon our busy mothers called for us to peel potatoes or change the baby or fold the laundry left waiting. We'd shake the grit from our towels, say our goodbyes, return to our homes. Only our damp imprints remained. Those shadow selves, with their girlish whispers of desire, their plans to leave the block behind.

Complicit

My father talks on the phone, long cord spiraling from the wall to wrap his arm like a bracelet. His low, warm voice is a sound I haven't heard before. He takes clean glasses from the dishwasher and places each one on a mom-lined cupboard shelf. An action I haven't seen before. I'm in our hallway, scratchy carpet beneath my legs, a book in my hand.

Wednesday evenings my mother processes data alone in a locked business office, feeds secret combinations of ones and zeros into a wall-sized computer for hours. After she returns, she comes into my bedroom and bends down to kiss me goodnight, to ask if I've said my prayers. I don't mention my father's voice.

I listened well from the hallway, Mom's graying poodle in my lap. Long afternoons of aunts gathered at our kitchen table, lipstick-rimmed coffee cups in their hands, my grandmother slicing apple pie. She tells them, her voice leaning in, how a man shouldn't be left home alone at night.

My Siblings and Me

I was the youngest, the only girl. The boys were several years older than me, and our other sibling, a bottle of Pabst, was nestled in between us. Cool and amber, smooth and caressable. We called him P for short—but only if our parents weren't around. Mother called him "Pabby" and kept him close to her, let him ride in the front seat of the Buick even when it wasn't his turn. P never had to do dishes. Our parents said they didn't have favorites, but we knew better. Things took a turn for the worse when our middle brother started sharing secrets with P and doing what he could to gain our mother's ear, to get into the front seat with her the few times we left P home, alone.

Under the Sweatshirts in My Closet There's a Metal Box

That Ziplock bag of screws in the china cabinet drawer
belongs to something important. Just let it stay there.

A dash—only a dash, mind you—of sriracha sauce
heightens the flavors of anything that simmers.

Don't believe my journals. Everything in them is true,
but the truth was momentary. I forgot to add addendums.

Stargazer lilies are my favorite. I'd like them
at my funeral. Or, better yet, given away

like the tabs of valium and sticks of Juicy Fruit
lingering aunts shared at funerals in my youth.

Blue. Bruce Springsteen. A nice blend or a cabernet.
Walking with friends. Oceans not mountains. Dark roast.

I admit to some satisfaction imagining loved ones
needing to medicate themselves from my loss.

Grandma kept bags of change hidden in a heater grate.
"You never know when you might need a train ticket."

Take a coffee mug home. Each one was my favorite.
Tell a story about it. No one will know if the story is true.

Unsteady Claims
of Belonging

Bill's cottage is in Sturgeon Bay, at the beginning of
Wisconsin's thumb. My husband, our two daughters,
and I drove up whenever schedules allowed. We'd store
our groceries and suitcases and head for the water—
the girls already fussing about my insistence on life
jackets—to see how the lake had changed since our last
holiday. Every visit the same as the others.

A short walk down the road past a smidge of woods
there was a burger joint called The Moorings. Our
place to start, a totem to our arrival, it seemed a way of
declaring *now* we are here. I can't recall if the burgers
tasted good, or if the fries were special. I do remember
the dining room's clouded glass walls, the lake a pane
away on three sides, the bar behind us. The smell of long
days in the sun hung in the air, along with the sounds
of glasses and bottles clinking, trays being set on tables,
voices calling to new arrivals, the happiness of sailors
and cottage owners and weekenders all mixing it up.

We weren't sailors, nor could we honestly call

ourselves weekenders. We were more like twice-a-yearers lucky enough to tie up to a brother's cabin. I wanted to believe I could moor my family to this borrowed place, could declare a restaurant table tucked in a building built on water ours. But ritual and habit are unsteady claims of belonging, dependent as they are on all manner of causes and conditions.

Leaving Home

St. Joseph, St. Anthony, and Elmo go for a Walk During Mercury Retrograde

Our ongoing home selling adventure owes something to Saint Joseph, the patron saint of home and family. The house went up at what, to me, seemed a high price, but which fell in line with our area's comps. We hit the MLS (multiple listing service) scene on a Thursday morning and expected to field our many offers on Sunday evening. Everyone said this is what would happen.

A few showings. Some positive comments, some neutral comments, no offers.

After a week without an offer, the pressure from loved ones to inter St. Joseph upside down and within reach of our For Sale sign became nearly unholy. Rationally speaking, I felt almost certain St. J was not spending his celestial coffee breaks scanning for coffined figurines of himself, but I was not immune to the external—or internal—pressure. Generations of dead Catholic relatives seemed to hover around me shouting—in a most unangelic way—*just bury the damn thing*. Relatives accused me of enjoying my worry when I didn't take action after that first sad weekend.

Once we rounded week two with no buyers in sight I began avoiding anyone who knew our house was for sale. I even considered purchasing a St. Joseph Statue Home Selling Kit from Amazon ($6.75), but decided to gather more information before pulling out my credit card.

Soon I was visiting The Church of Google. Apparently St. J likes flowers. And he should be facing the house or facing the street and only turned right-side up if the house sells. The practice of stashing St. Joseph is either from the turn of one of the centuries or the 1970s. An article I discovered in the *Arlington Catholic Herald* quoted the interviewed priest as saying (I'm summarizing a little), this is weird shit and congregants should knock it off. Burying Catholic medals representing saints is okay, but interring statues is a no-no.

I felt vindicated and joyfully called a cousin to bring her up to date on all of our real estate news. I did admit I was disappointed we weren't having the same house selling luck as everyone else. She reassured me this was for the best. We were in a Mercury retrograde and nothing would go well until we cycled through to some other planet alignment.

Between our buyerless house—closing in on three weeks at this point—and hourly reminders from neighbors about how quickly the house would sell and how rich we'd become, as well as my ongoing Mercury retrograde/St. Joseph anxiety, I was more than ready for a weekend away with girlfriends.

We gathered at a large property filled with prairie grasses, wild flowers, and plenty of wine. I shared my angst—including a text from my sister-in-law entreating me to take ecclesiastical action before our weekend open house. I texted her back that her brother—my husband—was now in charge of all St. Joseph-related discussions.

Several non-Catholics in the group became confused and wondered if Saint Anthony could be of help in this situation. Sigh. After expressing dismay and incredulousness at their lack of understanding for how the world works, I provided education about St. Anthony's role in finding lost objects. He simply needs to be called on for help. Personally, I have found him effective at least eighty percent of the time. I do not subscribe to the rather too friendly, "Tony, Tony turn around, something lost must now be found" ditty I've heard acolytes intone. I'm more of a believer in respectful pleading in my discussions with saints. Bottom line: no, Anthony wouldn't be of help.

Despite the bucolic setting, I continued to fret about how the saints and Mercury retrograde fit into my dilemmas and asked a buddy to walk with me. I hoped she'd help me sort it all out. However, she got distracted by the lost items conversation and, believing herself helpful, told me her strategy for finding lost items comes from Sesame Street's Muppet monster, Elmo. Picture the last place you had the item and look there, he apparently advises. My friend swears by this technique. She didn't know if entombing Elmo upside down next to a For Sale sign would help sell a house though.

Three weeks into our plight, I got the longed-for call from our Realtor. A reasonable offer had been made. We were saved. My husband, Bruce, returned from errands and we did the happy dance when I told him the news. Once the excitement wore down we went for a walk. Bruce said he had something to tell me and he didn't want me to be mad. I took a deep breath while waiting for him to continue. That afternoon he'd driven to a religious store and purchased a St. Joseph statue. He'd opened the package, read the directions on proper placement and magic words, and then tossed everything on the back seat of his car. He didn't say if St. Joseph rested upside down or right side up on the car seat. And I'm not going to ask.

Here's What Happened at Our House over the Past Thirty Years in No Particular Order as Well as What the Home Inspection Revealed When We Decided to Sell

We attempt to give the client a comprehensive, clear-cut, unbiased view of the home. Page 1

We scrubbed the already clean walls and floors and refrigerator shelves of our first house the same day we signed the paperwork making it officially ours. It's not as if anything looked different when we were done, but by the time we said goodbye to those who had come to help, something new had begun. The smells of pine and bleach would welcome the paid movers hauling in our furniture the next morning and already there was a memory to share.

The purpose of this inspection is to identify 'MAJOR' problems associated with the property being purchased or sold, although minor items may also be mentioned. Areas, which may be of concern to us, may not be of concern to the client and some items, which may be of concern to the client, may be considered minor to us. Page 1

We replaced the brown shag carpeting with whitish Berber. Relatives helped us remove the old carpet by rolling the cut sections and dropping them from the second-floor window. Then we replanted the bushes outside the second-floor window. My husband replaced hollow pine doors with good quality six-panel oak ones. We installed new windows to reduce winter drafts. One day a visitor noticed our daughter's eyes didn't track together. There were months of visits with specialists. I changed diapers. I rocked babies and calmed them with Springsteen songs all through the night. One time we went to a prenatal exam, but the fetus didn't have a heartbeat anymore. We drove home from that appointment. One day became another day. I made soup. Kids went to school. Kids went on play dates. Kids joined the Girl Scouts. We made phone calls from a wall phone set into a wood and ceramic decorative case with a drawer for note paper. We attached a longer phone cord and added a second line in the bedroom. We had an answering machine. Then we all had cell phones. Then we got rid of the house phone. It was winter and the kids from the neighborhood slid down the small hill in the backyard.

It was summer and we bought a blowup pool. It was the next summer and we bought another blowup pool. It was summer and we had all the neighbors over for a cookout. It was winter and we had a Solstice party. It was fall and I composed a poem inviting relatives and friends alike over for another holiday party. We cleaned up from parties. Clank of dishes as we put them in the dishwasher. Hum of the vacuum.

Items in the home can and do experience failure without prior indications. This report is a snapshot of the condition of the home at the time of inspection. We cannot determine if or when an item will experience failure. Therefore, we cannot be held responsible for future failure. Page 4

Saturday lists of chores for the girls and any friends who stayed overnight. Little Cindy at the door borrowing this or that for her mom. Men in the driveway doing some project. Sound of chainsaws. Well-dressed men or local high school kids ringing the front doorbell hoping to sell God or gift wrap or popcorn in a tin. That time Polly pulled the TV over on herself. Replaced the furnace, replaced the water heater. Added an air conditioner. Took a bath. Meals in the crockpot, the smell of bacon, grease on my shirt. Made liver. Once. Band-Aids on wet skin, Band-Aids on lotiony skin, Band-Aids that led to tears. Ambulances called—well, only one, but several considered. Started meditating. Decisions made in the kitchen, decisions made in the bedroom, decisions made when walking down the hall. Bee stings. Brain surgery for Bruce, eye patches for Elizabeth, always the odd rash on Polly.

... it appears to be in serviceable condition at time of inspection Page 12

Took the brown paneling off the basement walls. Painted the hallway, retiled the bathroom. Calked. Patched. Speaking of retiling the bathroom, there was that time we moved a loose tile. One tile led to another and suddenly the wall rained carpenter ants. Got a second mortgage. Made lunch. Sliced an avocado. Went tent camping. Bought a camper. Camped. Sold the camper. Pitted cherries. Once. Had Ginger and John over for the weekend. Watched TV. Raked the lawn. Had Realtor over. Had a stager over. Straightened the For Sale sign. Made a list of items to sell. Reduced prices of items we didn't sell. Loaded up boxes, loaded up arms, loaded up the car. Loaded up.

Leaving the Neighborhood

"And yesterday I found out I had a metal plate in my head," one neighborhood guy said to another as I walked past. "From the dentist," he replied to the listener as I ambled out of earshot.

I'm paying closer attention now as there's only a month left until we move to another house in another community. Earlier in the week, for example, while soaking in our backyard hot tub, I mentioned to Polly, my visiting adult daughter, that I hadn't seen Owen's dad in a long time. Owen was one of her neighborhood friends back in the day. I never knew the dad's name (or don't remember it), but he was one of the constants on our block. Always walking his golden retriever. In later years, he'd stop and lean on the mailbox post across the street from my house before continuing up the hill towards his own. The lean once went on for so long I thought I should offer help, but between the idea and my feet moving he began walking again. In our hot tub, huddled down to chin level to avoid mosquitoes, I told Polly I've been filled with memories the last few weeks and how the recognition that Owen's dad hadn't been around sprang from that. I couldn't honestly say how long it'd been since I'd seen him.

"That's because he's dead." Polly told me. Either a heart attack or cancer she thinks, she's not sure when, and by the way, Owen is married.

I reflect on this news for days with an odd, false sadness for something lost I hadn't realized I cared about. I ask Polly about his mom—I don't know that I've ever spoken to her, just seen her drive past for years— hunched close to the steering wheel, cigarette in her mouth, wild hair. There were rumors of drinking. Polly doesn't know if she still lives in the neighborhood. It seems to me—a flash of image—that in the last year I've seen her drive up past our house in the morning. An odd time to drive that direction—only the parents on pickup duty go up the block before school hours, everyone else is headed out of the subdivision for the day. I remember wondering if she had taken a third-shift job.

The next morning I'm up early. Sitting on the front porch bench where I pretend to meditate with my first cup of coffee and sure enough, I see Owen's mom amble past with that dog Owen's dad always walked. She saunters right past without stopping to lean on the mailbox post or look in my direction—just keeps going in the direction of her cul-de-sac and toward whatever life she now leads.

My new neighborhood will be quieter than this one. More birds, less cars. This is literal as I currently have a highway in my backyard, but I wonder if quieter means better. There won't be a sidewalk with its parade of people and dogs. The bus won't squeal to a stop to fetch kids in the morning. I won't get the mail straight from the postman's hand, won't spread mulch on these particular flower beds each year, or freshen the blacktop every few years; won't walk around the block nodding or good morning-ing to neighbors mowing lawns, monitoring toddlers, carrying this or that from the car to the house.

There won't be a chance to tell that guy I knew about the plate in his head, how he fell from a roof right here in the neighborhood. He told me the story himself—many years ago and on this very block when I stopped to pet a puppy he was walking, a gift to help in his recovery.

Dear New Owner of Our Home

Twice, ground wasps have taken over old chipmunk burrows. The first nest, near the raspberries (which are multiplying like crazy), my husband discovered while mowing the grass. He got stung several times. Let me just say ambulances, should you ever need one, arrive quickly in our neighborhood. The second nest appeared a few weeks later near a bush by the downspout—the downspout next to the solar panels (which will work much better once you get those dead ash trees down). I spotted the new nest during my now-routine walk-about scanning for such things. That very warm, humid evening, the stars just beginning to show themselves, I bundled in snow pants and mud boots, parka with the sleeves pulled tight around my wrists, and sprayed the chemical heck out of the murderous thing. No further problems.

I've planted lots of perennials, but you won't find many. The ground is rocky and the chipmunks are numerous. Trudy, from next door, has threatened to shoot them for the last thirty years. That's only been talk as far as I know. There's a slope to the yard as you move towards the back—yes, this can make grass cutting a bit difficult, but come winter it makes for a fine sledding hill. It's easy to keep an eye on the kids from the kitchen window while doing dishes or heating milk for hot chocolate. Or while slicing carrots to throw in the crockpot; the smells of beef and bay leaf circling towards the kids as they enter all winter-loud, their movements large and so different from the soft entrances of summer. Cold air rises off them as they toss hats and mittens looking for mugs of something hot, snacks of anything.

I digress. Didn't even mean to mention the crockpot. But I should say something about how tricky the smoke alarms are. They'll go off with the slightest hint of warmth. If you stand on the third step of the staircase, one hand on the railing and the other waving a dish-cloth you'll get the screeching to stop quick enough. Then you can take the battery out while you finish supper. When you go to bed, and are finally all snug in the soft blankets, you'll remember about removing the battery and can head back down the stairs to reattach.

I'm told you have a young daughter. We've raised two here, so I can say some things about how that might go. I think it's good to have a two-story home. Your daughter can stomp away in anger for a satisfying distance on occasion. And the time it takes you to march up or down the stairs might be enough to prevent you from saying stupid things you'll regret later. Not always though. Ah, well.

If your couch is perpendicular to the living room windows, you'll be able to keep a close eye on the neighborhood comings and goings—who walks which dogs at what time, what cars belong up the block versus down the block and who drives too fast. And then there is the upstairs master bedroom closet (a walk-in). Oh the sleepless nights I'd write in that closet—shirts hanging above me, shoes all around me—when the girls were young and I didn't want to risk waking them! The pen across the paper. The warmth of the heat register—I know, such an odd place for one. The release of what I didn't even know needed release. Then the relief of sleep. Have a nightstand close to the bed for your phone and a glass of water, maybe a book. You know how it is, if the phone is far from your reach it's sure to ring in the middle of the night.

Sorry about the walls. When we moved in here wallpaper was everywhere. Chickens. It didn't come off easily. The lower bathroom is our fault though. We added spackling paste for texture, but as you can see it was much too thick and now changing colors in those deep cracks is a process. The neighborhood has turned over since we moved in thirty years ago. There is a new crop of kids. They ride their bikes down Willow Drive without helmets, sometimes with no hands on the handlebars, sometimes looking down at phones. I won't comment on this—anything said just makes me sound old.

I guess you'll find your way. Your own frustrations and your own spots to curl up on those sleepless nights. Maybe you'll attempt a garden. Watch out for the chipmunks, they like to burrow.

Various Ways to Leave

I thought this was about leaving my home of thirty years for the last time. How I pulled shut the door handle, heard the click behind me, knew that when the door next opened it would be with the new owner's hand. But that hasn't happened yet. I'm plotting my goodbye scene now, fingers poised above the keyboard as my future life unfolds. Scent of a neighbor's wood-fire drifting through the window and sounds of geese in formation calling their own goodbyes.

I remember the last time I visited the brother who drank too much, how I memorized the sound and feel of his door opening. I didn't bother knocking. He hadn't answered his phone in days so it was that type of visit. He sat low in his chair, smoking a cigarette, his dog quiet at his feet. "I'm not going to a damn hospital," he said by way of greeting. "No one asked you," I said by way of response. We shared the lunch I brought. Chicken and rice of course; smells of home floating from the fry pan, even the dog showing interest. Afterwards I cleaned his kitchen, scrubbed the sink, put the useless leftovers in his refrigerator. I held the front door open for an extra breath before I left, just staring at the back of his head. Then I pulled the door shut behind me, correctly guessing I wouldn't ever arrive there again.

My husband replaced our traditional doorknob with a numerical keypad a few years back. When I'm anxious I fear I'll forget the code and be locked out. I could probably safely share it here. Our home's new owner ... I mean *the house's* new owner will want to create a new way in, will have her own reasons for choosing each particular number.

Earlier this year I vacationed in a house near a lake. Each night I walked a mile to where the road ended and the lake began, in order to watch the sunset. Sometimes carloads of other people already waited. One evening everyone left right before the sun made its final hurrah into the water. That's when my favorite time begins, when the sky changes with every moment. So much is missed by leaving too soon. I've heard others talk about a green click of light when the sun leaves for the day. Friends of mine claim to have seen this many times. I've never witnessed it myself although I'm always hopeful.

In just a few days I will leave the house I lived in from thirty to sixty. The kids and dogs are already out. The furniture is gone, and the place has been swept clean. Thirty years is a lot of time to have lived somewhere. My hand will rest on the door handle while I take a last look around. Then I'll pull the door shut and I'll listen for that final click.

Alternate Faiths

Alternate Faiths

At the conference we—social workers in search of cheap continuing education credits—learn excessive gambling is an addiction that literally changes the brain. Many researchers believe excessive slot machine play alters the mind. The dopamine hit from pulling the lever and watching the spin of the cherries and lemons so strong that winning becomes an unwanted interruption to continuous play in the most seriously affected. This is the sad end from the video clips we see of middle-aged players lining up tokens of luck (Beanie Babies, rosaries, rabbits' feet). These same players refuse to believe that near misses on favorite machines won't predict future wins. Each machine, we soon learn, is completely random with every new spin of the reel.

Machines care nothing for prayers uttered or promises made; the results are determined with the pull of the lever, before the spin even begins.

There is a video in the afternoon. The reenactment of a financial meeting led by Gambler's Anonymous members. "Are you sure? Have you told us everything?"

The savvy questioners grill the gambler over and over as they ask about other bets, other debts. "Yes, yes" he replies, until he doesn't, until he equivocates, and head bowed, confesses once more.

Didn't we all gamble to get to this room this morning? Any morning? Gamble that all the other drivers would stop at red lights, would stay on their side of the yellow line, would follow, would follow, would follow. So much faith we have in strangers.

Why I Became
a Social Worker

Because the rhythm of my mother's week revolved around Friday afternoon appointments at the beauty shop. Because I wanted to know what women whispered about, what they promised not to tell. Because I didn't think I could cut hair. Because all week my mother's rolled and teased hair—hair we kids weren't allowed to touch—fell further into shapelessness. And then, finally, Friday revival at my aunt's beauty salon. Our place of sanctuary, place of family, place of women, place where hair could be touched—if touched correctly. We checked in with the well-coiffed, red-nailed receptionist, hung sweaters or jackets on the coatrack's noisy metal hangers, greeted the stylists at their stations, took in the soap opera unfolding across the black-n-white television mounted in a corner high above the sinks. Waited for the shampoo girl to call us over. Lay your head back, another towel under your neck?, scooch up a bit, there, that's good.

Because my mother had a standing appointment. Fridays at 2:00 comes to mind, although I might be wrong about the time. But coveted Friday is true and I crossed my fingers for perm days: for long, humming afternoons of predictable sounds, low conversations and laughter, the bell above the door, the cash drawer, the broom sweeping everything away, the certainty of an appointment next week—even if just for a set and comb out. The sharp, wakeup smell of perm solution and hair spray fresh from the can, the cigarette smoke, the staff office I could lounge in since I was family, always food and an ashtray on the table. Open containers (macaroni salad, bean salad, coleslaw with mayo) from the Sentry's or the deli next door. Forks, plates. Everything shared. Bottles of twenty-five cent soda slid from the machine in the back hall. Half-cups of black coffee, pink or red lipstick prints on every rim. The week's problems laughed off, everything forgotten, the mirror unfolding someone better for the next week.

Because my cousin, the owner's daughter, cut the hair off each of my baby-dolls. She did this because she could, because she was bigger, because she was practicing the trade. I didn't practice—not on baby dolls, not on other people. My mother didn't mess with her own hair, except for hopeless mid-week efforts to pick and pull at the flat spots. I barely combed mine, never trimmed a crooked bang, never experimented with measuring damp hair through my forefinger and middle finger until stragglers poked past begging for a trim. I never dared claim that power; something, it seemed, only professionals should do.

Because there was alcoholism and affairs and arguing at my house but at the beauty shop my aunt smoothed my mother's shoulders, caught her eye in the mirror, held her gaze, massaged her scalp with kind fingers, then let the wide-toothed comb gently flow through the wet hair until the ratted and tangled parts all fell away. Because of the salon's cadence, the bell above the door, the constant phone, heels across the floor, the scissors, the clippers— all of it a safe background jumble when I begged for a quarter, when I spun on the chair, when I asked for the broom and swept away the brown and auburn and blonde hair until everything became clean again.

Because of all those Friday afternoons of curlers and bulky bonnet hair dryers, each with its attached chair and hood of warm air that drowned out sound. Only a quiet time for dozing, or reading magazines, or watching the complications of our muffled shows remained. Our family problems cut and rolled out below the drama of soap opera characters, their own layers of issues carousing in the bleached and colored air of the salon. Too soon the mirrored reflections of beautician and client brushed everything into its perfect place until the chair slowly swiveled, a handheld mirror helped reveal all sides, and the weekly blessing bestowed, "There now. That's better."

How the Water Holds Us

My brother Bill tells me to "put the thing on the thing" and hands me a rope before he shuts down the runabout's motor and allows momentum to carry us to his pier. I lean into his words, whisper his instruction to myself, consider the direction of his eyes. I follow clues from our past—years of making meaning from his distracted language, for example—and tie a half hitch around the dock cleat when we come to a stop. The boat settles and bumps gently against the protective fender.

Never jump into frigid water, another brother once told me. He'd been playing basketball on a sweltering summer day and, adrenaline still pumping, sweat still sweating, leapt into a hose-water cold swimming pool and became ill: his stomach cramped, his limbs heavy. Ease in slowly, he often said afterward, leaving out information about depth. His need to save me trouble, I suppose, but I leaned into the story's middle—that brief airborne interval between hot exhaustion and expectation, before the water momentarily claimed him, sobered him with unwanted lessons about acclimation.

—

In Costa Rica, rip current postings frame the beach: what to avoid and how to swim to safety. As usual, it's wisest not to struggle or panic. Swim slant to save yourself, wave your arms to find help. Fighting just leads to exhaustion, to being carried further and further away. When swimming, I tried to keep my daughter close— near enough to touch. Even with posters I couldn't discern what the lifeguards easily spotted: the broken wave pattern, the line of churning debris, or oddly, calm areas indicating danger. If the phantom current reached for us, I'd pull her to me. Keep her from going out to sea. My unnecessary plans to save her have become my clearest memories from the trip.

—

Back in the day, we kids loved to shout underwater in my friend's backyard pool. It was a game we played to divine what the other said, our voices muffled and impossible. The legs of brothers and sisters all around us, the silent bouncing of their language from above. When we came up for air, we both declared victory over the muddled words, our recollections as unpredictable as the water.

—

Turns out I needed a cleat hitch to tie up my brother's boat. The half hitch with its two loops twisted one way then the opposite way wasn't enough to hold us for long. I misread the signals. No one fell when we crossed from boat to pier though. Boat. Pier. One not much different than the other and both so dependent on water. The right language another way to steady us, to keep us safe.

Things I've Forgotten,
Just for Today
(and Possibly Tomorrow)

Teeth brushed, bedtime T-shirt on, blankets snuggled close, and sinking into day-is-doneness, I'm sure there's one more thing—something to do with an email or an appointment. I just can't quite isolate it from my bedtime head swirl. I do know Charlene, one of my mindfulness students, says she heard tell of a vortex in Lake Mills, Wisconsin. That's what I'm mostly thinking about. I wrote her information down weeks ago to look up. Otherwise, forget about it.

——

My husband, watching the news earlier in the evening, didn't even acknowledge me when I said I had something to tell him but couldn't remember what. "I probably will when I drive away," I said as I kissed him good-bye before heading out to teach my meditation class. And I did.

—

Being in a car cued the memory I suppose. Earlier in the day, I canceled the insurance on my daughter's hand-me-down Monte Carlo currently stored in my father-in-law's garage. If a heavy-limbed tree smashes through the roof and lands on the car, or a lightning strike makes an inferno of the garage, our comprehensive coverage will still cover the damage. However, if in anticipation of garage destruction we move the car elsewhere and it's damaged, we suffer the loss.

—

Two articles caught my attention in this week's *Time* magazine, one reviewed hybrid cars, and the other, on happiness, suggested I consider life without social media and send my laundry out. I placed the yellow-stickied magazine next to my plate before supper and thus remembered to share both articles with my spouse.

—

The insurance guy now needs proof my daughter is abroad before he'll cancel her car insurance. Days will stream past, as perhaps he hopes, before I connect daughter, an unknown document, my scanner, and his email.

—

I watched a video on spoken word poetry—so I could cross that item off my to-do list. The list is always on the counter next to my purse, near the hook for my keys. Last year I made a New Year's intention to memorize one poem per month. By the time Lent arrived I'd given up.

—

To better understand the illuminated and shadow attributes of my personal collective unconscious, I pick a daily archetype card. Today I chose clown. *How much do you laugh?* the vibrant card asks. Do you laugh with joy or to mask other emotions? I may have forgotten to laugh today but not on purpose, there just wasn't an opportunity. I picked this same card—or the card picked me—yesterday. And once last week. A curious occurrence, considering there are forty-eight cards in the deck. I'm trying to understand what I need to learn about laughter. The answer, I believe, rests somewhere between sticky notes, the dog's vet appointment (oh oh), and expired mayonnaise.

—

I fed my spouse expired mayonnaise because I forgot to check the date (I had an inkling, but never near the fridge) before starting supper and because ketchup on a BLT seems wrong. I fed my spouse expired mayo because adding mayo to the grocery list slipped my mind, and I couldn't recall if expired mayo was bad or, like aspirin, could be used for years unless it smelled like vinegar. That, I'm pretty sure, is what my mom said concerning aspirin. I never buy aspirin. There's something about a disease. Here's the thing: I didn't necessarily forget to purchase mayo. Mostly I wanted to avoid the dreaded mayonnaise/Miracle Whip conundrum. I know any attempted quick trip to the grocery results in overlong staring at the shelves, wondering if it's mayo or Miracle Whip I need. The actual miracle being no one would know which I'd purchased as I'm the jar opener and dressing spreader in the family. I tell them what I want them to know. Perception is everything someone once said.

—

I couldn't find my phone when I arrived at meditation. That surprised me. As well it should, since I later realized I'd had the phone all along—simply tucked underneath my purse instead of in my purse. I rushed through my preparations for leading our mindfulness-based class. Everyone else forgot to come, or chose not to come. Perhaps they were in Lake Mills visiting the vortex. I meditated alone; immersed in the present moment and a new day's supper plans. I gathered the donation I'd placed in the basket to inspire others and felt compensated. Then I went home to my list, curious to find out what I should do next.

—

I can't find the page in my notebook where I wrote down the vortex information.

I Felt Myself Give Way

In the alley behind my childhood home we kids moved between jump rope rhymes and Red Rover invitations until the street lights called us home. Dads kept the garage doors open in the after-supper gloaming, their version of family time while they puttered and fixed and waxed. Each house on the block a mom-ruled island of requests and denials with all paths leading to a hot supper on the table at five o'clock. We raised tents in our backyards, defended them with crab apple wars fought between drying towels and sheets; raked leaves into piles, tossed footballs. We shoveled the front sidewalk in winter, weeded between the cracks in spring, and tanned from one end of the block to another in summer—too impatient to stay in one place for long. Our chalked hop-scotch frames and miniature four-square courts decorated the walk between storms. We followed the rules, jumped from number to number, never left the block.

—

Middle school. We're at Nan's house. She is the youngest of somewhere around seven kids, so something is always going on. This one afternoon, the light no big deal, just clear or maybe cloudy, we are in her backyard. There's a tractor tire. I'm about twelve at this point and the tire is as tall as I am. I never questioned why a tractor-sized tire would be in Nan's backyard. That's just the kind of house she had. A place where anyone was welcome and a peanut butter sandwich could always be found. Dollars to donuts her mom was sleeping on the couch this particular day. And the aunt who lived with them must have gone shopping or this memory would include details about getting yelled at. A tree of some type was in the backyard. Laundry poles are likely. The line between them hanging with towels and a shirt or two, items forgotten when a phone rang or meat frying on the stove was remembered. And the driveway sloped. Perfect for rolling down kids stuffed in a tire. I had a vague sense of knowing this wasn't a good idea, so I wanted to do it. Climbing in tires and rolling down driveways pushed me towards bad, out of the nice girl category and towards tough. I wanted to be tough; the same reason I'd begun leaving St. Gregory's playground at lunch recess to smoke cigarettes with Nan and another friend. Anyway. There's the memory of hands balancing the tire upright, helping me in, running alongside me. The air inside the tire is warm, like a cocoon or nest.

—

In our Catholic all-girls high school I leave Nan behind or maybe she leaves me behind. Much later I learned her path involved running away and an underage stint with a traveling circus. A Google search reveals she eventually married and had children. As for me, well, there were more nuns to contend with, a locker full of detention invitations, late nights, fast cars, and underage drinking. I had left the block.

—

If anyone wanders through Google looking for me, they'll find evidence of college attendance, a page of incorrect addresses, a trajectory of marriage and children, the occasional speeding ticket. Professional jobs. Business casual attire. Attendance at all things that should be attended. Eggs for breakfast, meat and potatoes for supper.

—

We gather for Easter with extended family. The ham is fully cooked, unlike Thanksgiving's turkey. My married nephew's no-longer-new baby rules the day. He lifts his arms and we gather him in ours, he points and we follow. Such a simple thing, small warm body pressed into ours, one arm out straight, fist curled, pointer finger pointing. He gets whatever he wants: smidges of bread, a stuffed bunny, numerous Goldfish crackers. The scene plays out over and over through the long holiday afternoon. All of us pleased to be chosen by him, to be the one to follow his point to the desired object, to place the reward into his open hand. A year from now we will demand *pleases* and *thank yous*. We will want to shape his simple desires into a negotiation. We will insist on compliance.

I like to walk through my subdivision in the dusky light. A liminal time when the neighbors might still have their curtains open and I can see movement in their kitchens—the opening of a cupboard, the bent over form of someone finishing a task, the staccato flashes of reflection from television news. On this one night—later than dusk, stars already out, I remember the soft crunch of new snow, cold hands in my coat pockets, taste of wood smoke in the air—I felt myself give way. I continued along the safe sidewalk of course, but something had changed. As if I'd become porous and the walls of the homes had melted away and we— all of us living in the neighborhood—were one, just going through our evening as if connected, as if happy. Too soon I was back in my own driveway, opening my own back door. The houses grew their walls again and we all separated into our own selves, doing our own routine chores. Then I was kicking off my shoes and my husband was calling out, "You back? Can you get the dogs out? They've been waiting."

So I put the dogs out and hung up my coat and began to make our supper.

My Brother Tells Me

"You don't have to eat eggs only at breakfast. There are no rules." That's what my brother, the rule breaker, said to me. His tone was mocking. He liked to call me while driving. I'd hear the clink of ice cubes when he took sips from whatever he was drinking. It, the rule breaking I mean, the letting go of shoulds, didn't do much for him. Not in the end anyway. But he had some good days; days I often envied. Bonfires made long before dark in his home's backyard deep in the northern Wisconsin woods. Hours to watch how the deer bent for corn at sunset. Time for this as he hadn't been to work, or pleased a wife, or soothed a child. No need to carefully cross items off of a list. Long hours to listen to animals call warnings through the forest; first crow, then squirrel.

On what will be my final visit to his cabin, I have to wash his dishes before I can make him lunch. He watches me from his one comfortable chair; unlit cigarette in one hand, drink in the other. The remnants of scrambled eggs cling to his plates and flatware. He tells me he doesn't remember making eggs.

His words about rules shadow me. One morning, a few days after my visit, I soak in my hot tub while the rest of the neighborhood works. Dried leaves fall like rain. I'm the only one seeing this I think, and wonder who to tell. I will eat ice cream before lunch. Each swallow like something breaking open in my chest. A transgression, its worth yet to be weighed.

Towards Midnight

Towards midnight I take the dogs outside one last time, they are old and no longer need leashes—the dark is enough to keep them in their yard. I follow them into the driveway. The Big Dipper usually shows its September self right above and between the across-the-street neighbor's two big maples. But on this particular night the sky is a full-on blanket of clouds. A glow of lightning appears when I look for the constellation. Not a strike, just a glow. The only one despite how intently I stare—until the dogs circle me, done with their explorations and ready for bed.

What I Know From My Spot on the Couch in a Borrowed Cabin

Silence is best. Particularly the silence of a house not my own. No layers of to-dos audible in the air around me. Just the gentle crackling of the Franklin gas stove set next to a loose-fitting window.

Rising heat drifts through the cool air and makes the lower pane ripple, beyond that an uneven breeze causes the dried red maple leaves to bobble. I know pine cones will fall from the Tamarack onto the front stoop and need to be swept away just as I'm sure I won't actually take the broom from wherever it is and complete this task.

The kink in my back will be fine if I stand and move around, but I won't get up until the pain is strong enough to prevent all other activity. I'll eventually need a nap today but will walk instead. This is my way, to deny myself, to put off what I want. Right now there are the sounds of laptop keys and my fingernails tapping against the coffee mug. The gentle click of the stove. And the sound of leaves rustling through their autumn changes—if only I would open the door to hear them.

How to Convince Yourself It's Still Meditation If You're Drinking Coffee

Begin slowly. Breathe deeply twice and then let your breath come naturally. Without judgment acknowledge that your first thoughts are about coffee. Let those thoughts drift away like beans through a grinder.

—

Recognize (again, without judgment) how great it is you are willing to sit outside in all kinds of weather these days. Bow to yourself for this. After pouring your coffee, pause for a moment to feel the warmth of the cup, the steam as it reaches to caress your face. Move outdoors to the wicker bench you have begun using for morning meditation. Arrange the red indoor/outdoor pillow you added for butt comfort just right as you settle.

—

Create a mudra of hands pleasantly cradling your coffee mug. Consider how holding and occasionally sipping from said mug is really no different than gazing at a candle or other object. Chant opening words as opening words makes it official you are now meditating. Realize that the line, "may we be free from hunger and discord" practically blesses the drinking of coffee while meditating.

—

Taste your coffee. Do so mindfully. Are there floral notes? What is the aroma and bouquet—oops, note that you might be thinking about 5:00 meditation. Return to right here, right now. Sip. Are there chocolate undertones, have you added enough creme? Resist returning to the kitchen for just a dash of cinnamon to heighten the flavors. Be with the discomfort.

—

Breathe. Feel your shoulders move down and away from your ears, feel your body relax into the bench (although keep your spine straight). With your chin slightly tucked and your gaze soft, manage to notice the woman from down the block who walks her two labradoodles at this time every day. While she and the caramel one wait at the corner, the black one rolls in the dewy grass. After they have passed, wiggle the slight ache from your back. Try not to think about what to make for supper. Although it's okay if you do; just let the thought pass like kidney beans and tomatoes added to yesterday's chili.

Make sure your legs are uncrossed. Feet on the ground. Feel the breath of the earth coming up through your feet and into the hands holding your expensive-yet-chipped pottery mug like a favored child. Recognize the thin webs of spiders in the dying pine's branches, the way the bees land on each flower, drink, and leave.

—

End your time with another sip. Notice how the taste changes as the coffee cools, how the color of the liquid seems to sink into itself. Bow to this good yard. Recite your closing words. May the hearts of all beings be opened.

Walking the Labyrinth

Two women sit on a stone bench in the middle of the labyrinth, a spot for chanting or prayer or at least wishful thinking. West Bend's Labyrinth Garden Earth Sculpture's seven circuits are lined with all manner of plants native to Wisconsin, creating a sensual and peaceful path for the seeker searching for inner wisdom—or at least a diversion to her day. There is no way out once beginning the spiraling, unicursal, hope-fully mindful trek to the center.

On the first circuit I visualize letting go of all that needs letting go. However, I'm haunted by an image of our COVID-19 positive president removing his protective mask, to expose, if not literally, then at least symbolically, all around him to illness. I am aware this same image is a symbol of strength to many, a pictorial statement indicating he—and our country—will not be beaten. For all I know the women on the bench may hold this opinion.

The second circuit weaves me back towards the laby-rinth's opening instead of closer to the middle. The unexpected turn reminds me of something that's been nagging at me: I'm staying at a friend's cabin for a week and couldn't get the Franklin stove to work when I arrived. A neighbor was called. He arrived, recognized a loose wire, left to get tools and returned with his Trump-hatted stepfather. I recoiled, felt my hand on the door tighten, my breath catch in my throat. I'm embarrassed that I let a hat cause such a cascade of emotion, even if I'm the only one who knows. The man fixed the wire so I wouldn't have any more issues during my stay. He was gracious as gracious could be—as was I. Except on the inside.

By the time I enter the third circuit I'm surrounded by autumn dried plants, although the black-eyed Susans and bee balm still throw off some color. I'm now close enough to the two women to hear the murmurings of their conversation. To recognize the rhythm as easy, as chat-like. I admit I'd like them to leave before I arrive in the middle.

Loving kindness towards others is my desired mantra for each heavy-footed step I take on the fourth circuit. Instead I dwell on current events, on politics, on all those I wish gone in one way or another—from their jobs, from this space, or just from my thoughts.

The circuits are smaller now. I'm much closer to the center where I can say a prayer or meditate a moment, or at least feel refreshed, lightened of some burden. But the middle remains crowded by the two women. I act as if there's a rule prohibiting our being together.

I keep my head down as I walk the second circuit to give them privacy, but they call to me. One of them asks where I got the brochure in my hand. I answer and they thank me. Soon I complete the final circuit and stand in the center, right behind them. I don't feel more at ease or unburdened in any way. I don't think I can blame the news or even the women relaxing in the spot I wanted for myself. After all, I'm the one who paid barely any attention to the lilies along the paths, the spacer stones labeled with messages of love, or the careful tending this place requires.

I'm the one who can try walking back a different way.

The Mystery Continues

Keeping Things Nice

My stroller is metal. Maybe a yellow, but a faded yellow—I'm far from the first inhabitant. There is a tray with a raised rim for my hands or a doll, a footrest for my feet, and a roof for shade. I'm sitting, leaning forward instead of relaxed against the backrest. The day surrounding us is clear and the nearby houses are quiet.

Lyon's Park is behind us. I'm sure of this. My internal compass is continually oriented towards the park and who might take me there. In my mind the red-slatted wooden swing with a bar that lowers to keep me safe emanates from the strong arms of whoever is behind me pushing and pushing until I can kick towards the sky and holler whatever I want to holler without being shushed. Perhaps we've left the park earlier than I wanted or perhaps this walk is a quick pre-nap cruise to settle me down. Trees and fences must be present as we pass one house, the entrance to our alley, another house, but whatever objects I insert into this scene are just pencil-lined shadows, as if I'm recreating a sketch of what a neighborhood should look like. I'm wearing

85

boxy, off-white toddler shoes. They've also seen other inhabitants and are much polished and buffed. Hideous. A brother pushes the stroller. I'm guessing it's Dale. He's only seven years older than me. Bill is a full nine years older and probably knew how to wiggle out of this chore. But my memory can't really see who's behind me, squiring me.

Here's the heart of this thing: I decide to remove my feet from the footrest and scrape the toes of my shoes against the cement as we make our way towards home. Not only will this create drag, lengthening our forced time together, but will remove the layer of polish so carefully applied by my father.

I picture him with one hand in the shoe to hold it steady, the other applying the polish—the sponge applicator covered with bright white paint erases all the mistakes, all the signs of other kids. A bottle of Pabst is on the end table next to him and he says, "keep these nice now." I know, even at the tender age of whatever, that scraping the tops of my shoes along the cement is a very big no-no. I also realize I won't be blamed. It will be the stroller pusher's fault. So. A clear decision is made. A reckoning of pros and cons. I—for a forgotten reason—will take an action that results in consequences for someone else. This is my first memory. This recognition of my power.

At Grandma's House

Don't go to bed with gum in your mouth. One of two things will happen: you'll accidently swallow the gum and have it stuck inside your intestine forever or you'll choke to death.

Sleep on soft goose-feather-stuffed pillows for the best night's rest. The geese that provide the pillows are kept somewhere in the way backyard. It is best not to ask questions about the geese. Somehow you know this although you don't know how you know this.

Sylvester is the ghost Grandma calls on to keep us in line at bedtime. He knows if you place your gum on the bedpost for safekeeping. And he hovers if you need to pee in the red coffee can kept for such emergencies in the small closet off the upstairs landing so make sure you really have to go. Yes, there is a toilet downstairs, but it is only for daytime use. Sylvester will also have something to say if you lean back on two legs of those good kitchen chairs used not only by Grandma but by her parents and other dead relatives before her.

Joanne Nelson

The house on Sixtieth and Cold Spring Road is endless with rooms upon rooms and Grandma is likely to appear from anywhere. She is as frightening as Sylvester with her solid and unpredictable body. She might be carrying pointy goose feathers that really aren't soft at all or even a temperamental bag of kittens. Mind you, I haven't seen her carry a bag of kittens but there are rumors. And based on family legend—she is the eldest of eleven, more if you count stillbirths and early disease—she is capable of doing what needs to be done. Her father was a drinker, but who wouldn't be with all those kids? Her mother, Julia, served the church, and had longed to be a nun.

Oh, how I loved to cover the ground nests of bees in Grandma's rolling front yard with an old pickle jar, watch the poor things fling themselves at the glass so close to the real world, yet not.

88

It's Picture Time

So. About a week ago I'm at a goodbye party. The host, a photographer by nature, announces, "Picture time." He's artfully arranging various groups and I'm placed with the evening's honoree and my spouse. I might be the youngest one at the party—my craggy, worn spouse is within reach of Medicare, and the woman leaving is a good twenty years older than me.

We huddle in, smile big, create flat surfaces of our guts. The photographer raises his camera, fiddles a bit, lowers his camera, looks directly at me and says, "Push your chin out. It fixes neck problems."

My spouse and the honoree pull away just the slightest bit, and from the back of my head I sense the party attendees chatting behind us begin to stare. The birds in the trees outside the window hush themselves. I look longingly at my glass of red wine sitting alone and lonely just out of reach on the dining room table.

I don't quite understand the chin out thing and I didn't know I had neck problems. I gamely jut my head out as far as it will go, drawing the corners of my mouth downward with the effort and causing my eyes to bug out. "Not quite that far," he suggests. I try again, this time contorting my lips upward. Apparently this fixes my glowing, mountainous neck because after only a dozen or so more tries he declares, "that'll do" and heads off towards the stove. The camera is now a depressed looking lump hanging from his slumped shoulders.

Later, standing in a dark corner of the host's home digesting both potluck casserole and my neck fiasco, I remembered a similar, less public surprise from years earlier. A friend had come over for coffee. During our conversation she mentioned how distraught she was about a huge wrinkle going straight down her forehead, right between her eyes. I looked. Wowza, now that she'd mentioned it, the split down her forehead was cavernous!

"I never noticed before, you can barely see it," I said. And I thought, *Thank God I don't have a wrinkle like that.* After she left, I went to the mirror for confirmation. Nope, no worries, I didn't have the huge frown line that announced her arrival. I had two. And no amount of eyebrow lifting or gentle attempts at pulling my skin back behind my ears—I considered duct tape—made the image in the mirror any better.

Once safely home from the goodbye party, I tell my visiting daughter what happened. She demonstrates the gentle way one glides a chin forward, notes how this simple act lifts and tones; she suggests I also put the tip of my tongue on the roof of my mouth for photos. I ask no further questions.

In my bathroom, finally alone for the first time all evening, I bravely take a look at my neck. Huh. There's been a transformation since last I took a good look at myself. My neck seems to have been replaced with my grandmother's when she died at the ripe age of ninety-seven. Or, maybe from a few weeks after she died. I try pushing my chin towards the mirror. Well, yes, that is better. Several decades are magically removed from the hills and valleys of what was once a smooth road of a neck. I resolve to keep my chin jutted out at all times; why waste this miracle only on photos? And, I decide, much as I like the person moving away, I won't be asking to see the party pictures anytime soon.

Sick Day

Sick with something common in my lemon-colored bedroom in my super big bed with all the pillows I can find tucked tight around me and the view to our backyard with its picket fence and the sidewalk my father will walk down as soon as the sunlight starts to fade. To the side of the yard, just out of sight of my bed, are the three crab apple trees I play under on better days. In front of me is my desk with the real desk blotter with the cushioned sides that I've drawn on instead of using all the paper I've been given like I'm supposed to. For now, there is a rimmed metal TV tray—gold edging and flowers on a black background—within my reach and on it are *Little House* books from the library and saltine crackers that I've been eating too many of—loving both the salty crispness of each bite as well as the mushy mushiness when they've soaked in a bowl of Campbell's chicken noodle soup with the so-thin noodles and odd-colored chicken. The TV tray also holds a handkerchief, one of my dad's big white squares—the nice ones with grandmother-embroidered edges are not for actual use.

This particular handkerchief has snot in the corners, dried and crispy—better than when the handkerchief is damp and fresher snot gets on my fingers and the side of my nose. Sounds from the black-and-white television in the living room float down the hall to my bedroom although I can't quite make out if it's *Let's Make a Deal* or *As the World Turns*. My mother comes in, places a hand on my forehead, adds water to the glass vaporizer at the side of the bed. She wipes a finger full of Vicks on the drip cup to further warm and soothe the room. Soon the vaporizer gurgles and bubbles hot steam I'm to stay away from so I don't get burned. But I reach down from my bed, put one finger and then another above the hot moist air, wanting to know how close I can get before pain drives me away.

In the Kitchen

I was in the kitchen. My eldest was fifteen or there-abouts. Her choices frightened me. They weren't bad, not really. I can say that now. But they were all in the direction of bad and several of those she hung around with had already slipped the slope. It was a lonely time for me—even though I worked a lot, made most of the meals, schlepped everyone everywhere. I remember leaning against the sink, towel in my hand, fretting ... And next being surrounded by my grandmother. Not a physical presence or touch from this grandmother who'd died several years earlier, but just a total being with me. And she said—no, no, said isn't right—she let me know that everything would be okay, that I could settle myself. The whole experience was so, well, full.

Other People's Houses

College. My roommate and I are invited to a friend's lake home. Cool. Neither of us has friends with lake homes in our outside-of-college lives. Although my grandmother did have a trailer on a lake in Portage, Wisconsin. The lake home is a beautiful place with a real bathroom and bedrooms enough for guests—so different from the trailer my grandmother had on Long Lake. At Grandma's trailer we peed in a Folgers' coffee can at night and in an outhouse ("watch out for snakes before you sit down") during the day. We slept on always-damp, pollen-infested couches through the long nights. Nights of fitful sleep interrupted by the calls of owls, the barking of coyotes, the sound of tinkling in a can.

At supper, made by my friend's parents working together, neither drunk as far as I can tell, there is discussion of local political happenings—primarily agreement, but sometimes disagreement in the same even tones while our friend takes another helping of salad and grinds fresh pepper over the mixed greens.

No one has been told to shut up or even hit upside the head. There is lingering around the table after the clinks of silverware have quieted. I'm unsure of what to do in this peaceful gathering where no one longs to leave the table. I have a strange desire to tell someone their opinion is wrong. Because I said so, that's why.

My Neglected Gods

What the Dog Said

Our current dog sleeps in the living room. I don't have to see him to know this. These days he is nearly always on the couch resting his sore joints and poorly functioning heart. If I go anywhere near him he'll lift his head and stare into my eyes. Despite our fourteen-year relationship I've just begun to notice this. And I wonder if his visual lock on me is a new habit, or if I was too unaware, if scales needed to fall from my eyes.

What's going on, a variety of online sites tell me, is about Oxytocin. We are both releasing the love hormone with this gaze, with the way I feel pulled toward him more and more often, with the way I seem to anticipate his needs (desire for a different pillow to sleep on, a blanket smoothed or moved, the need for an extra treat). How like me to finally recognize him so close to the end.

Each Hazy Element

This is about my dad's basement den, his toy car collection, and my engagement; these three things circling my memory for weeks now, each hazy element looking for connection.

First, my engagement in the late 1980s. My boyfriend of six years finally asked me to marry him. He scheduled a weekend getaway, made restaurant reservations, even got down on one knee. Despite our many years together, the decision to join our lives in front of God and everybody made me giddy.

I couldn't wait to tell my father. We weren't close, and I didn't think he'd desire a role, but in this new blush of potentiality, my existence was corrupted by glossy images from bridal magazines. Dad and me as photo opportunity.

"Can't tonight," he said when I called and asked to stop over. They were busy, maybe another time.

No, no. That's okay. Nothing important.

We met up the next week. My enthusiasm dimmed— as if a space had opened between my excitement and this particular story that I could fill with scripted assumptions for years to come.

We sat in his basement den the night of our scheduled visit. Its paneled walls were crowded with handmade display cases filled with his collection of hundreds of toy cars. A separate vitrine housed decanters of whiskey-filled porcelain Indy 500 race cars (their value questionable since my mother had broken the seal of each before handing them over as part of their divorce settlement). The driver's names stenciled on the cars felt like old friends: Foyt, Unser, Andretti.

These were the drivers I rooted for on Sunday afternoons when my family gathered around the television, window shades pulled down to prevent glare, and watched the races—any conversation angrily hushed, the spell of the engine roar not to be broken. I savored these long afternoons spent together. My time devoted to coloring in the Indianapolis 500 activity book my dad had bought me, careful to stay in the lines, looking up if the announcer's voice rose in anticipation of an accident.

Little of the actual sharing of our engagement news with him remains clear. Just our phone call, driving to his house, and being in that room with all the cars. What fogs my memory is all the fictions I created about the visit. My dad, I worried, questioned our need to interrupt a perfectly good evening with something best accomplished over the phone. But I'd wanted to see his expression when we made our announcement—

although I don't recall what I wanted his expression to be or what it actually was. It's as if, in his small den, we each sat in a different car headed in a different direction: my dad with a need to drive away, me with a need to arrive.

His marriage to my mother had been hastily scheduled and quickly arranged. He went AWOL from his army unit to attend—although his own father refused to come. And this current marriage? Dad shared his nuptial news in a phone call weeks after the event; like describing a hiccup in his schedule, it was certainly nothing requiring a visit or an announcement.

Happier stories existed. I'd recently come across a 1964 photo of him at the wheel of his restored Ford Model A, a just-married cousin waving from the rumble seat. I wonder if he thought about that day while we discussed our plans. He'd have detailed the Model A with tenderness. I knew this from a childhood of watching him prepare for parades and car shows: the round can of Turtle Wax always close, the refusal of any offers of help, the way he'd lift us kids into the rumble seat to avoid getting the slightest of fingerprints on the Brewster green finish.

"You care more about those cars than us," I'd often heard my mother say. Perhaps serving as chauffeur for the bride and groom had afforded him the opportunity to quiet the charge. I think he relished his separation from the din and emotion of wedding well-wishers—sequestered in the cabin of his Model A, the newlyweds behind him all but forgotten.

Except for the toy cars lining his walls, the den is empty now. The furniture has been passed onto others, the television given away. A combination of mustiness and mildew hangs in the air, dust gathers wherever it can. My dad is dead and won't celebrate my thirtieth anniversary or learn of my daughter's engagement. His wife lives in an apartment and no longer drives, the couple from the rumble seat divorced long ago. So many arrivals and departures from his room of toy cars. Now it is only the possibility; no, only the desire to drive away that is left. Such a shame really to have all those wheels remain so still.

Open Windows

Five of us are spread across two picnic tables discussing air flow. We wear jackets for the first time in months. According to research on viruses carrying respiratory droplets, if you open windows across from each other and add a fan either blowing in or out you'll be fine. If you turn the furnace's humidity setting to forty you'll be fine. If you add a carbon filter and a HEPA filter—the combination is important—you'll be fine. If you add a room to your home that is not on your furnace system and you hang out in that room with a space heater you'll be fine. Unplug the space heater when leaving the room. Do not open the windows if the air quality is bad due to uncontrolled fires in your area or if locusts have arrived. This open window thing is, of course, dependent on the side of town you live in. Screens are important. Be wary of bees. Some of this is not based on research but is true just the same.

What Godliness Is Next To

Jung defined neurosis as "a neglected or repressed God." We are at the mercy of the energies we once gave to God of gods apparently. This energy is now just sublimated, misplaced. "Our ancestors believed in gods," Jung said. "We believe in vitamins—both invisible." And yet (or perhaps just "and") it is Jung who hung a plaque above the door to his home and whose gravestone reads, "Bidden or unbidden God is present."

—

A sky stripped of clouds is next to godliness; the blue surrounding us without beginning or end. But God appears best in the nighttime. Once, while attending a high school Christian youth camp, several of us climbed atop our bus's flat roof to watch the night sky turn. Our youth minister used a flashlight to point out constellations and to tell their stories. Cassiopeia, Perseus, Andromeda, all waiting for us to call on them. That's not exactly what the youth minister said, but it's what, unbidden, opened up in me.

No Reason to Remember

1966. My brother washes and I dry. Every night. Unless we have been smacked and sent to our rooms for a supper infraction. (In which case there is the god of crayons and clean paper, my desk next to a window facing three crab apple trees.) But on this regular no-reason-to-remember evening, there is my brother washing the Melmac dishes and me standing on a kitchen chair to stack each plate away in its correct cupboard. There is the loud scraping of pans being shoved against each other so they fit in the rarely used broiler drawer below the oven. And best of all there is the music coming from the radio on top of the refrigerator. WOKY's Bob Barry playing the top forty hits and telling us who to follow, what to believe.

Things I Rely on to Be Okay

Gum on airplanes, a bottle of water, something to
read, a way to exit. These are the things I rely on to be
okay—on planes, certainly, but also in summer crowds,
at conferences, and in post office queues. My midlife
versions of a blankie, or totem; some charm against the
unknown.

More totem than blankie for me in childhood: I had a
monkey. A hand-made one, I mean. Red butt and red
smile, heavy black thread lashes I could pick at, thin tail
stuffed with old pantyhose, the beige fabric poking out
from a rip in the seam. A loyal smiling face, and the
faint smell of Lady Esther face powder, Folgers coffee,
and morning bacon all knit into the lifelike thing. Not
literally knit; really just two socks sewn together—the
red heel of one now a butt and the heel of the other now
a smile. Lifelike might also be incorrect.

Still, a stuffed monkey as protector. My grandmother's
gift as symbol of belonging, as special. I came across
them again as an adult, machine-made and sold with

stuffed animals everywhere—large enough for cuddling or shrunk to the size of key chains, even hung on Christmas trees as ornaments. The same, yet different: no soul in their nylon-free bodies.

Growth Potential

My grandmother had bags of coins hidden throughout her home for "just in case." My other grandparents kept a careful notebook filled with the cost of milk and gas and what income came in. My mother hid money in her underwear drawer and kept files of mutual fund statements going back for years. My father has another wife with her own children. We have a financial advisor with an SUV and vanity plates that read "counselor."

A Digression about Purses

The monkey-sewing grandmother's purse contained yellow Juicy Fruit gum. A light-colored purse, it belonged to the beige family, and the smell—once she opened the catch—sang of juicy fruitiness. My other grandmother's purse was heavy, black, and sounded of loose change. That grandmother had a thin wallet for bills, and clumps of wadded-up Kleenex, but it's the dusty change I remember most; the dull rattle of it against the bottom cardboard strip that gave the purse form; such a hopeful sound in the days of penny candy. Her husband, my grandfather, carried his change in a flower-like squeeze pouch he kept on his dresser.

No smells come to mind about Other Grandmother's purse, although textures do: rough-edged bus tickets, wrinkled receipts, old keys, fuzzy stuff from the zippered sides. Change though, that's what I cared about. This grandma, the one with the heavy, black purse, gathered her extra quarters and dimes in plastic bags tied off with bread wrapper twisties and hid them around her house. We'd find the bags in her dresser, under a heating grate, deep beneath embroidered napkins in a china cabinet drawer. Enough, she told me, for a train ticket from Milwaukee to her family's home in far-off Winona. Always have enough for the train, she said. You just never know.

The Stories We Tell

I have convinced myself that holding a coffee mug, even sipping the nectar contained within, is an appropriate way to meditate. The gentle aroma, that mix of sweet, spicy, smokiness surrounds me briefly as I pour, so like, I imagine, the day to come. My hands cup the warmth, fingertips touch in a personal mudra. I am open to receive. I have also convinced myself that checking emails during hymns while attending Zoom church is acceptable—or it's what I do anyway.

At Any Given Moment

Foot off the brake, hand barely resting on the Subaru's steering wheel while driving north on 41 today. There's minimal traffic as I cruise up the eastside of Wisconsin to the peninsula of Door County and I have plenty of time to study the yellowing oaks, red maples, anti-abortion billboards, and porn shop advertising along my route. I want to experiment with letting go, with letting the car's automatic systems for speed and steering take charge. If I take my hands off the wheel for more than ten seconds, beeps and flashing orange lights require me to change my ways.

—

There's a new writing center being built across the street from where the residency I'm attending for the next ten days is located. The center was scheduled for completion in May, but now, in September, the landscaping has just begun. Paths remain muddy, trees wait to be planted.

A walk in the afternoon after unpacking: saw a deer. We surprised each other and both froze; after a brief assessment we went our separate ways. The hard rustle of drying leaves followed us, only our scents lingering behind.

—

Drama from home is unfolding throughout this first afternoon of settling in. My father-in-law has been admitted to the hospital for pain. As the hours pass the phone calls seem to gain weight. The words themselves become concrete chunks that threaten to topple me. I learn he has a bladder infection. Decent news; easily treated. I learn the cancerous tumor in his colon has grown, even doubled. Not unexpected news. The tumor has broken through the abdominal wall. Game changer news.

—

There is a pandemic moving through the world. We wear masks for protection from each other. Today I have seen black masks, rainbow masks, and white masks with red lettering. My mask is blue to match my eyes.

—

Don't come home, my husband says, there's nothing you can do; *I* can't even stand to be here. Our two elderly dogs are asleep on the couch, he tells me. I could have guessed that, knowing them, knowing exactly where they can be found at any given moment.

To an Old Dog

Getting lost in corners is not a good sign and praise be you don't do this yet, nor do you stand on the wrong side of doors waiting for them to open but then again how would I know if you were and just now I remember the two times last week I opened the basement door and there you were on the topmost step seemingly unconcerned about your spot in the world—although now I wonder, can there be a wrong side of a door? Still, you often lean against me for a good scratch, sniff the air for loss, cushion yourself along the other dog who lags a year or two behind you on this journey, and gaze into my eyes with such love anytime you are awake, that look of yours my rescue from all the ways we leave.

Roadside Tarot

Modern Arcana

My brother had a car accident once. He'd been arguing with his second wife while driving on a busy expressway. The traffic slowed suddenly. He didn't use caution, hit his brakes too hard and spun across the lanes. No one got hurt. But the car came to a stop facing the wrong way. This, it seems to me, was often his story (work problems, alcohol problems, a third divorce, general problems of living)—facing the wrong way, I mean. Maybe the accident skewed more metaphorical than he realized. I picture a modern tarot card. Major arcana. Automobiles, a spear, something upside down.

Reversals Interrupt Flow

Today I leave a writing residency I've spent months longing for. I leave after a mere twenty-one hours to manage a loved one's illness. It's what I'll want to remember doing, I tell myself. Notice how this is different from leaving out of concern or love or even duty. I gift myself with time for coffee before leaving. Sit at a dew-damp picnic table and look into the yard's fading summer colors; imagine the week the woman I won't be, might have had. Glory in the words she would write, the sketches she would sketch, the meditations .... And then I leave her behind, finish the packing, wash the coffee cup, get into the car, turn the key.

Divination

One time, years ago, I drove to my brother's home deep in the woods just to see if he was alive. I remember the feel of my hand on his doorknob, how I let myself in without knocking.

Another time I drove with a friend to her apartment so she could pack her possessions before an abusive boyfriend returned. Both of us jittery. Both of us stared hard down the street of the clear, seemingly friendly day each time we stepped outside her door with another box.

Fog, on three different occasions. That time I drove alone, I inched ahead praying the road continued in front of me. Another time, driving with a friend, we had to stop. She got out and walked ahead looking for curves. The other time I was swimming when fog rolled in. I lost my way (the water was calm, shallow) for what felt like too long.

Roadside Tarot

Caution written in black letters on large orange triangle signs. One on each side of the highway. Bright blue day, no bumps in sight, no high water danger, no construction workers about to begin a project. Just the two signs. What am I to make of this? This highway tarot card without nuance or guide.

I talk with various family members several times after I drive past the caution signs. Just the push of a button to connect, but I fumble for the phone, for the right button. Look up, fumble, scan the highway, fumble, etc.

Action is required for those caution signs to appear. Someone wakes up, has coffee, loads a truck. Double checks the location, hauls the signs out of a county vehicle and places them across from each other. This somebody also has loved ones and dreams; possibly a place they'd rather be. Perhaps they see meaning in this job on this day, perhaps they see the signs as personal. I get lost when downtown Milwaukee looms with its multiple signs and exits south and west. Twice I have to exit and reenter the expressway. Still, nothing bad happens. Sometimes we get lucky.

Luck

At one point during my journey, a white car comes to a complete stop in front of me for no discernable reason. Left lane. Right lane remains open. As I pass around the car I see a woman, face turned towards me as she speaks to a passenger. They are having their own issues I imagine, although the sudden stoppage seems like a tragic invitation to join them. Luckily I was paying attention, despite talking on the phone—discussing something important related to a loved one's crisis. Unfortunately the details of the conversation have been forgotten.

An Overarching Theme

Orange cones appear alongside the road in another section of the highway on my drive home. No signs warn of this brief lane closure. Unless, of course, I was looking down instead of scanning the suggested twelve to fifteen seconds ahead when the warning came. "Drive safe," we say, although no one said it to me this morning. But what does *drive safe* mean? Do we say it for the driver about to leave or are we saying it as a self-protection—*I told her to drive safe.* Is it the thing we want to remember saying?

Alternate Readings

I've had the experience, mostly at night, of a car speeding up behind me and flashing its lights on and off—signaling I should move over or speed up I suppose. But what if that's not it? What if despite the sudden arrival, the apparent urgency, I'm wrong? What if the message isn't for me at all?

Acknowledgements

Grateful acknowledgement is made to the editors of the following publications in which portions of this book first appeared, sometimes in slightly different versions: *Brevity, Poetry South, Citron Review, Inscape, Mindful World, 8142 Review, 50 Give or Take, The Other Journal* as well as recordings for *WUWM'S Lake Effect* (Milwaukee's local NPR affiliate).

Special thanks to Paul Corman-Roberts, teacher of fine classes and guru of organization for his help in this collection's creation and to Joanna Penn Cooper, another fine teacher, for the ideas that led to many of these pieces. I am forever grateful to Jerod Santek and the staff of Write On Door County for writing residencies during which this work was fretted over, spread out across rooms, and even completed. Many thanks to Bob and Gina Magnus for the gift of time and inspiration at their lake home. I'm also lucky to have spent time at the Prospect Street Writers House where friendship and the love of writing gather at every meal. V, your kindness, your generosity, and your cooking are much appreciated. Thanks also to Kim Suhr of Red Oak Writing, and my Moving Pens roundtable. Our time together keeps me motivated and the pen moving. And much gratitude to Linda Michel-Cassidy who has once again helped guide the words into the right spots.

I am blessed to have an amazing group of friends who offer support, guidance, and lots of laughter. Thank you!

The key to all of this is, of course, family. Much love to Chris, Alex, and Sam.

Lastly, endless thanks to the always kind and forever patient folks at Vine Leaves Press. From initial acceptance to launch day and beyond, the team of Jessica Bell, Amie McCracken, and Melanie Faith have answered oh so many questions, given spot-on guidance, and provided an atmosphere of collaboration. Cheers, and cheers again, to each of you.

Vine Leaves Press

Enjoyed this book?
Go to *vineleavespress.com* to find more.
Subscribe to our newsletter:

Printed in the USA
CPSIA information can be obtained
at www.ICGtesting.com
JSHW021156140823
46475JS00005BA/228

9 783988 320162